Exploring
Caves
Journeys into
the Earth

Exploring
Caves
Journeys into
the Earth

By Nancy Holler Aulenbach and Hazel A. Barton

with Marfé Ferguson Delano

NATIONAL GEOGRAPHIC SOCIETY

WASHINGTON, D.C.

Contents

Imagine

Imagine the thrill of setting foot in a mysterious world no one has ever visited. That's the feeling cave explorers, or cavers as we call ourselves, get every time we're lucky enough to find a cave or a passage that no one has ever entered. It's like the feeling the first man on the moon must have had, and it keeps luring us back to these dark, hollow, and frequently damp places beneath Earth's surface. We just can't wait to find out what lies straight ahead or around the next corner. Perhaps a narrow passage will widen into a large room filled with fantastically beautiful formations. Perhaps it will lead to an underground pool filled with unique creatures. A winding passage might head back to the surface, and then again, it might just stop.

Of course, we don't find unexplored places every time we go caving. Sometimes we visit the same cave many times, to survey it for a map, for example, or to photograph unusual formations, or just to share its beauty with friends. Cavers also study the wildlife underground, from bats that dangle from cave ceilings to microscopic organisms that live in cave walls.

To us, caves are like hidden treasure chests, full of all kinds of secrets just waiting to be discovered. We hope our adventures will draw you into the fascinating world of caves and inspire you to learn more about exploring and caring for them.

Happy caving!

In Mexico's Jaguar Cave (left) we release a harmless dye into the water to see if the cave connects with the sea.

Nancy Holler Aulenbach   Hazel A. Barton

Caving on Ice

For serious cavers, few things are more exciting than checking out the caves in a place they've never been before. So when MacGillivray Freeman Films (MFF) approached Hazel and me about exploring some of the world's most fascinating caves for *Journey into Amazing Caves*, a new movie they were making for IMAX® theatres, we were intrigued, to say the least. The people at MFF explained that the goal of the project was not only to capture the spectacular beauty of the caves on film, but also to conduct useful science in them. They were looking for experienced cavers who could handle the science as well as the intense physical demands of caving in challenging conditions.

Luckily, Hazel and I fit the bill. A lifelong caver, I specialize in mapping caves, studying their geology, and performing cave rescues. Hazel is not only an expert caver but also a microbiologist—a

As soon as Hazel and I landed on the Greenland ice cap (above), we could tell that the caves here would be unlike any we were used to. Descending into an ice cave (left) seemed like entering another world.

The ice cap is very rough and rugged. Huge spires of ice jut up, and deep cracks, called crevasses, slice into the surface.

scientist who studies microscopic life-forms called microorganisms. Hazel searches cave environments for unique microorganisms. She and other microbiologists believe the study of these tiny cave dwellers might lead to a cure for a deadly disease or to new theories of life on Earth and other planets. We both jumped at the chance to take part in the film project.

In late September 1998, Hazel and I headed north on the first leg of our adventure. Our destination: the mysterious ice caves hidden beneath the frozen wilderness of Greenland.

Greenland is the world's largest island, and most of it lies north of the Arctic Circle. A gigantic ice cap made up of moving fields of ice called glaciers covers nearly all of its surface. Over thousands of years, this ice cap has piled up, layer on layer. In some places, it may be a hundred feet thick; in others, many thousands of feet. Near the center of the island, it measures two miles thick! I expected the ice to be flat, sort of like a skating rink. But as I could see from the helicopter that took us from the airport to base camp, the ice cap is very rough and rugged. Huge spires of ice jut up, and deep cracks, called crevasses, slice into the surface.

In summer, the temperature in Greenland rises enough to melt some of the upper layers of ice on the glaciers. This meltwater, as it is called, trickles into streams, which gather into raging rivers that rush over the surface of the ice. Along the way, the rivers plunge down into the crevasses. As the fast-moving water surges through the crevasses, it hollows out caves inside the ice cap. I couldn't wait to get on the ground and into those caves!

Glaciologist Luc Moreau leads Hazel and me over the ruins of a horizontal ice cave. The roof is made of huge, precariously wedged blocks of ice. Heat from the sun can cause the blocks to melt and collapse, burying everything below under tons of ice.

When base camp came into view, I realized just how isolated we would be. We had flown nearly 40 miles out on the ice cap. Except for a few tents huddled together, there was literally nothing but ice as far as our eyes could see. When we landed, we met Janot Lamberton, a Frenchman who has gone deeper into ice caves than anyone else alive. Every year, he and his son, Mael, lead an expedition of scientists to study the Greenland ice cap and investigate the caves beneath its surface. There is a short window of time in the fall during which the caves can be entered safely. That's when the temperature has dropped low enough for the ice to refreeze, but it's before the harsh Arctic winter sweeps in, making the ice cap too cold to visit.

Although the Arctic air felt frigid to me, I soon learned from Janot that we had arrived during a heat wave. Melting snow made it unsafe for us to enter the caves; we would have to wait until the temperature fell and the ice froze hard. While we waited for conditions to change, we had the opportunity to get acquainted with the other members of the expedition and to learn some of the special skills we would need for ice caving.

I had caved in many kinds of caves, but ice caving was new to me. The French team helped us learn to walk and climb on the ice wearing sharp metal spikes called crampons on our boots. Crampons dig into the ice and help keep you from slipping. But you have to be extra careful when you're climbing with crampons on, because they can slice through your rope and send you plunging. We also practiced a horizontal rope technique called a Tyrolean traverse to get across a deep ice canyon. I'd done Tyroleans before, but never while wearing thick gloves and bulky cold-weather gear, and certainly never with an icy river roaring 80 feet below me.

One day Luc Moreau, the team's glaciologist, led us over a jumble of huge ice blocks that had once been the roof of a cave. Heat from the sun had caused the roof to collapse. It made me realize just how dangerous ice caving can be. Despite my eagerness to check out the caves, I was happy to wait until Janot and his team gave us the green light!

A rope is a caver's lifeline, so I always do a last-minute check before rappelling (right). Hazel zips across an ice canyon using a rope technique called a Tyrolean traverse (below).

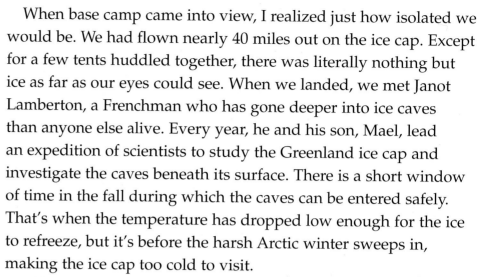

I was dazzled by the brilliant blue color....It was like being in an ice castle— a magical world where everything glistened and glowed.

A few days later a wind storm raced across the ice cap, bringing freezing air. Janot decided that it would be safe for us to explore a horizontal ice cave. Horizontal caves run more or less parallel to the surface of the ice cap. Luc agreed that the cave would be safe, but only until noon. That was when the sun would be strongest and could cause melting. If we stayed in the cave any longer, we risked being buried under tons of ice.

We trekked across the ice cap to the cave and rappelled into the entrance. Rappelling is when you lower yourself using a rope. As we made our way down a wall of ice into the cave, I was dazzled by the brilliant blue color. Janot explained that ice caves are blue because the ice reflects the blue wavelength in sunlight entering the cave. It was like being in an ice castle—a magical world where everything glistened and glowed. Sharing the magic with us as we ventured into the cave was the MFF film crew with the IMAX camera. Three years earlier the same camera had traveled to another extreme location—the top of the world's highest peak—to film *Everest*, which was also produced by MacGillivray Freeman Films.

Inside the cave, Luc pointed out the different layers of ice on the cave wall and how they alternated in color. The white layers, he explained, were from winter snowfalls. The blue layers were formed by surface water that melted in summer and then refroze. You can tell how old an ice cave is by counting the layers. Winter, summer, winter, summer, and so on. It's sort of like counting the rings inside a tree trunk.

Another day we explored Minnick, named for Janot's grandson.

The blue and white layers in an ice cave reveal its age. Each blue layer represents summer and each white layer, winter. The weight of the top layers crushes those below, so the deeper the cave, the thinner the bands.

Minnick is a vertical cave called a moulin, a French word meaning "mill." Only days earlier a roaring river was pouring into the cave, churning like a giant mill wheel and carving out a curve in the wall of the cave. Now that the temperature had plunged, the waterfall was frozen solid, and the cave was safe to enter—or as safe as a 500-foot-deep ice pit can be! Janot went down first. As he descended, he cleared the frozen waterfall of dangerous icicles that could come hurtling down like swords if our ropes hit them.

Even though I've rappelled into hundreds of vertical pits around the world, I was a bit nervous when I entered Minnick.

Chopping with an ax and kicking with his feet, Janot Lamberton clears razor-sharp icicles out of the way before the rest of us enter Minnick cave. Falling ice is one of the biggest dangers in an ice cave.

But as I descended, that beautiful blue light calmed me, and I felt very peaceful. When I had gone down nearly 200 feet into the cave, Luc put me to work taking measurements. The tremendous weight of the glacier, which is always moving, pushes the walls of the caves in on themselves each day. Luc would use the measurements we took in Minnick to determine how rapidly that cave was changing. While I worked with Luc, Hazel collected ice samples from the cave walls. She wanted to find out what kinds of microscopic life-forms—if any—live in the ice.

Although Hazel and I had met a few times at caving conventions, we did not know each other well before the expedition to Greenland. We quickly became good friends, as we shared caving adventures and camp life. Every evening

we'd bundle up and go out and lie on the ice cap and just look up at the sky. The aurora borealis, the beautiful northern lights, danced above us, providing our evening entertainment. When it was time for bed, we put on extra clothes to keep us warm while we slept. I wore down booties, silk underwear topped by two layers of polar fleece long johns, polar fleece gloves, and a hat that covered my face with rabbit fur. I slept in four sleeping bags, tucked one inside the other. All that was just barely enough to keep me warm. Every morning when I woke up my pillow was covered with frost.

Before we knew it our two-week stay in Greenland was over. Hazel and I said our farewells to Janot and the rest of his team and headed home. I would miss my French friends, but I was anxious to share my adventures with the second-graders I teach in Norcross, Georgia. Hazel was eager to get her samples back to her lab at the University of Colorado so she could see what she had found.

Skating at sunset is a great way to unwind after a hard day of caving (left). At night, moonlight casts a blue glow over our sleeping camp (below).

A Passion for Science

Unlike Nancy, who is quite comfortable dangling hundreds of feet above the ground, I'm not exactly wild about heights. But since I am wild about caves, I do whatever I need to to reach them. When *Journey into Amazing Caves* took us to a cave in the Grand Canyon, for example, that meant rappelling off the top of a cliff high above the canyon floor and then swinging into the cave entrance.

The only thing I love more than caving is science. In Greenland, my goal was to find out whether microorganisms called bacteria

Sometimes just getting to a cave is the most dangerous part of a caving expedition. In the Grand Canyon (left) I had to rappel down a cliff to reach a cave entrance. A helmet with lights (above) is essential gear.

This microorganism is a tardigrade, like the ones I found in the ice. It has been magnified 300 times by a scanning electron microscope.

live inside the glaciers at the top of the world. I suspected they would. After all, scientists have already found bacteria living deep within the ice cap covering Antarctica, the frozen continent that surrounds the South Pole.

While we waited for the temperature to get cold enough for us to enter the ice caves, I collected samples from the melted ice at the surface of the ice cap. Back at camp, I examined them under a microscope and recognized tiny creatures called tardigrades. Affectionately known as water bears, tardigrades have four pairs of legs and the remarkable ability to survive being frozen and unfrozen over and over. When the water they live in freezes solid, tardigrades enter a state of suspended animation, meaning they basically shut down. When the ice thaws, the water bears rev up again. They float to the surface and begin to move and eat and reproduce. Tardigrades are fun creatures, but my heart belongs to bacteria, which are thousands of times smaller. So I was excited when the temperature finally dropped low enough for us to explore the caves.

The deeper you go in an ice cave, the older the ice is around you.

After collecting ice samples from a cave wall (above), I returned to the camp's science tent (right). Mael Lamberton looks on as I examine the samples for signs of life.

If my samples contained living bacteria, these microorganisms would have sur-vived...more than two centuries.

The samples I chipped out of a cave wall 60 feet down are from ice that fell as snow about 200 years ago. As the snow fell, it would have trapped any bacteria living on the surface. Every year they would be covered by more ice. If my samples contained living bacteria, these microorganisms would have survived in a frozen state for more than two centuries. That's a long time!

Bacteria can be frozen and then brought back to life. Scientists use this technique to store microorganisms until they are ready to study them. Since my samples were already frozen, I just needed to make sure they stayed that way until I could get them to my lab in Colorado. At the Greenland camp I trans-ferred the samples into a canister of liquid nitrogen, which would keep them in deep freeze for the trip home.

Janot Lamberton helped me collect black debris called "space dust" from the surface of the ice cap. Scientists believe this debris comes either from space or from volcanic ash. Later, we rappelled into the cave at right and explored it on foot. The ice around us was 10,000 to 20,000 years old.

Ice caves are not the only kinds of caves scientists search when looking for unusual microorganisms. In the past ten years researchers have discovered hundreds of new microorganisms living in limestone caves all over the Earth. These supersmall cave dwellers survive on a diet of iron, sulfur, and other minerals. Along with other recent discoveries—such as the existence of heat-loving microorganisms in deep-sea volcanic vents—these cave "bugs" are helping scientists figure out how life may have first taken hold on our planet. One yet unproved theory suggests that life may have been brought to Earth inside rocks that originated somewhere else in our solar system, then traveled to our planet as part of an asteroid or a meteorite. These life-forms

The beautiful limestone formations in Colorado's Glenwood Caverns enchant me. Working with a team of three other cavers, I have explored and mapped more than two and a half miles of the cave.

I never imagined at age nine (above) that I would spend much of my adult life exploring caves. To map a cave (right), you need two people to hold the measuring tape and read the surveying instruments, and one person to record their findings and draw what the cave looks like. That's what I'm doing.

also help us speculate about life elsewhere in our solar system. After all, if microorganisms can live deep inside a glacier on Earth, then perhaps they can also survive under the frozen surface of Europa, one of Jupiter's moons, or in the polar ice caps of Mars.

Just as fascinating to me are the medical possibilities cave bugs may represent. There's a deadly new strain of tuberculosis, for example, that is very difficult to cure. As a microbiologist, one of my jobs is to find ways to treat people with this disease. Cave bugs may help me do it. These microorganisms are able to thrive in extreme conditions by creating some unique chemical compounds. Maybe one of them holds the key to a new drug that can be used to treat the disease. Researchers have already identified some cave bugs that have chemicals that appear to attack cancer cells.

Unfortunately, my Greenland ice samples were held up at the airport in customs so long that the ice melted. Even liquid nitrogen doesn't stay cold forever. The microorganisms, which love the cold, died before I could study them. Naturally I was disappointed, but as a scientist, I'm used to suffering occasional setbacks. The good news is that the French team has invited me to return to Greenland to do more research, so I'll get a chance to collect more ice samples.

At the University of Colorado I am part of a team of scientists who study unique microscopic life-forms. Here I am developing a gel that is used to study DNA.

I haven't always been fond of bacteria. The first time I heard about them, I was about six years old. My family lived in Bristol, England, where I was born and raised. One day a children's television show I was watching mentioned that every time you drink a glass of water, you swallow all these tiny organisms called bacteria. I was totally grossed out, because I imagined all these slimy worms and gooey, nasty-looking things in the water. For the rest of the day I refused to drink any water. I wouldn't have believed then that one day I would actually make my living studying bacteria!

My passion for science began when I was a teenager. I had a week's internship in a veterinary clinic. I liked it so much that I ended up working there every weekend for the next five years. At first I intended to become a veterinarian just because I love animals.

Over time, though, my interest in the animals grew into curiosity about all the diseases I saw at the clinic. I wanted to learn what caused certain diseases and how they might be cured.

During this time I also became involved with the other great love of my life—caving. I went on my first caving trip when I was 14, with an Outward Bound group. I discovered I enjoyed descending into darkness and crawling and climbing underground. In high school I was able to take caving as a sports elective. A teacher named Jim Moon, whom I think of as my caving mentor, taught a group of us caving and rope techniques in the limestone caves in some nearby hills. It didn't take long for caving to get into my blood. I was soon heading underground as often as I could.

After high school I attended the University of the West of England,

where I specialized in microbiology. The more I learned about how microorganisms, such as bacteria, can cause—and cure—diseases, the more fascinated I became with them. I made up my mind to pursue science as a career. The next step was graduate school, which brought me from England to Colorado. I was delighted to discover that Colorado is a great state for caving. Within days of my arrival I joined a caving club, and that helped me meet other cavers. I've been exploring and mapping caves in the western United States ever since.

Four years later I earned a Ph.D. in molecular microbiology from the University of Colorado, where I focused on *Pseudomonas*, a very dangerous kind of bacteria that can cause blindness and, in severe instances, even death if it infects people who are already sick. Currently, I am a research associate in environmental microbiology at the same university. I work in a laboratory headed by Dr. Norman Pace, a caver and a pioneer in the study of cave bugs. I perform experiments that examine the DNA of bacteria. I also study how bacteria get food and survive in different habitats. As a caver, I'm especially interested in bacteria found in underground environments.

To me, science and caving are a lot alike. They're both about the thrill of exploring. Whether you're performing an experiment in a lab or searching for exotic microorganisms in a passage deep underground, you never know what you'll find on any given day at any given time. Sure, sometimes you're disappointed or you hit a dead end, but there's always the possibility that you'll discover something wonderful.

> To me, science and caving are a lot alike. They're both about the thrill of exploring.

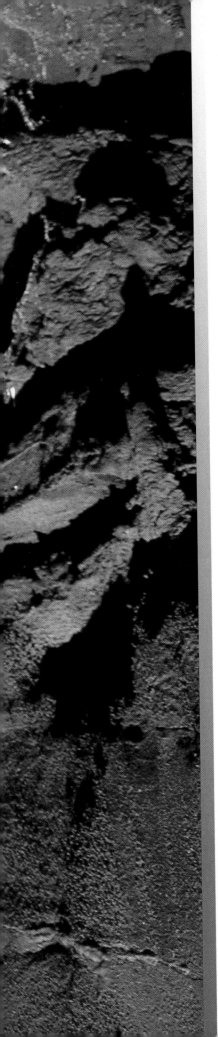

At Home Underground

Hazel jokes that if a cave creature is big enough to see, it's not really interesting to her. Microorganisms are her thing. I, on the other hand, prefer cave critters I can see without a microscope. I'm especially fond of bats, and I get to see plenty of them in TAG caves near my home in Georgia. TAG is a mountainous, cave-filled region located where Tennessee, Alabama, and Georgia come together. It takes its name from the first letter of each of these states. I go caving in TAG so often that I think of the caves there as my second home.

Several kinds of bats live in TAG caves. My favorite is a small,

I need a light to see where I'm going when I'm crawling and climbing around in caves. But bats—such as those that come out of Bracken Cave each night (above)— use echolocation to navigate and hunt for food.

When I was just a few months old, my parents carried me underground for the first time.

insect-eating bat known as a pipistrelle. Pipistrelles are real cuties. About the size of my thumb, they have little pink forearms and little pink noses and ears. Pipistrelles tend to be solitary, which means they hang out by themselves. Like other cave-dwelling bats, pipistrelles sleep during the day, dangling from cave ceilings. Toward evening, they wake up and fly out of the cave to hunt for food. Other kinds of bats live in groups ranging from fewer than a hundred to more than a million. The world's biggest known bat colony is at Bracken Cave, in Texas. Twenty million insect-munching Mexican free-tailed bats live there. Watching them swarm out of the cave at dusk is an awesome sight.

I've been around bats and caves almost all my life. When I was just a few months old, my parents carried me underground for the first time. I've been caving ever since.

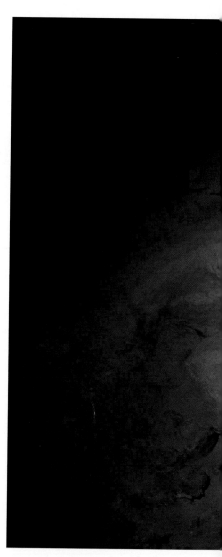

Caving was a family affair when I was growing up. Here I am at the age of five with my parents and two brothers, Oliver and Chris. On vacations, the five of us traveled all over the country visiting interesting caves.

Almost everything I know about caving I learned from my mom and dad, Susan and Cato Holler. My parents rigged a rope in a big oak tree in our front yard so my two older brothers and I could practice climbing and rappelling. Little did I know then that I would use similar rigging to practice for my expedition to Greenland. I wanted to get accustomed to handling a rope while wearing thick gloves designed for sub-zero temperatures.

My folks took us caving almost every weekend, and I loved every minute of it. Well, almost every minute of it. Once, when I was very young, I had to crawl through a tight passage. Clinging to the walls and ceiling of the passageway were thousands of crickets—big ones with long legs and antennae. When my helmet brushed against the cave ceiling, a mass of the insects fell on me. I can still feel them crawling into my clothes, terrifying me. To this

I am using a compass to map this cave. The measurements I take with it will be used to plot the directions of cave passages on a map.

day I'm afraid of crickets. I have to face that fear almost every time I go caving, because most caves are loaded with crickets. My caving friends tease me about it. Even I think it's kind of funny. I'm not afraid of darkness, tight places, or heights. I just have a problem with crickets, which are totally harmless. Maybe that's why I liked Greenland's ice caves: no crickets!

I am awed by how old some caves are. Most of Earth's caves, including those in TAG, are found in rugged limestone terrain called karst. In some cases, the geologic history of the rock goes back about 450 million years. At that time, parts of Earth that are now dry land were covered by warm, shallow seas. When the creatures living in these waters died, their shells and skeletons sank to the bottom, piling on top of each other in layers. Over time, the layers built up and eventually hardened into rock called limestone. (I often spot fossils of ancient sea creatures in the walls of limestone caves.) Eventually the limestone became dry land. In some places this happened when the sea level dropped, exposing the limestone. Elsewhere, forces deep inside Earth pushed the limestone upward, raising it above the surface of the sea.

TAG caves often have pools of water in them, so you have to be willing to get wet to explore them (left). Above, my husband, Brent, and I check out a tight passage in Hurricane Cave.

It takes two things to make a cave in limestone: water and time. As raindrops fall, they pick up a gas called carbon dioxide from the air and become slightly acidic. The acidic water seeps into cracks in the limestone and slowly begins to dissolve the rock. Over a very long time, the water carves out underground rooms and passages. After thousands or millions more years, the water drains away, and air fills the hollow spaces. A cave is born.

I love all the weird and wonderful stone formations in caves. They are created when water trickling into a cave picks up dissolved limestone along the way and redeposits it somewhere else, creating stalactites, stalagmites, and other formations. Stalactites are stone icicles hanging from a cave ceiling. Stalagmites look like upside-down icicles growing from a cave floor. All cave formations grow very slowly. It can take as few as a hundred years or as many as a thousand years for a stalactite or stalagmite to grow an inch.

These beautiful formations are quite delicate and easily broken.
A brief touch with even a clean hand can leave oils behind that
can bring countless centuries of growth to a screeching halt.

Imagine my excitement when Hazel and I were invited to join
the MacGillivray Freeman film crew on an expedition to a
beautiful limestone cave in a cliff 800 feet above the Little
Colorado River, near Arizona's Grand Canyon. Geologists believe
the cave began to form more than three million years ago.

As I rappel to a cave entrance in a cliff above the Little
Colorado River, I pause to enjoy the breathtaking view.
I'm wearing a seat harness with a device called a rack,
which helps me control my speed down the rope.

The film team figured out that the best approach to the cave was from the top of the cliff, 300 feet above the entrance. They built a huge winch that hung out over the canyon, then used it to raise and lower people and equipment. I chose to rappel down. As I swung into the mouth of the cave, a cameraman filmed me from a helicopter. The chopper was so close that I could feel the wind from its whirling blades.

The cave is huge, with big crystal formations all over its walls. As the Little Colorado River cut through the rock to form the canyon, it also cut into the cave, creating the opening we entered. As I stood at the entrance and looked down at the river far below, I realized that this cave would have been hidden forever if it hadn't been for the work of the river.

During our canyon expedition, I stayed in touch with my second-grade class via the Internet. Using a laptop computer, I sent them daily reports of my adventures. One day I was able to tie in my experiences with a classroom experiment. In class the kids and I had performed an experiment about saturated and supersaturated solutions. We kept adding sugar to water, watching it dissolve. Eventually the water became saturated, meaning it couldn't hold any more sugar. Instead of dissolving, the sugar settled to the bottom of the glass. The same thing happens in the Little Colorado River. It gets its milky blue color from a mineral called calcite, which is the main mineral in dissolved limestone. There is so much calcite in the water that the mineral settles to the bottom of the river and eventually forms mounds of layered rock called travertine. This is the same stuff that cave decorations are made of. I get a kick out of linking science class with real life!

Exploring caves is tremendously exciting, but it can also be very dangerous. One of the greatest hazards is falling, which

After gathering a water sample from the Little Colorado River, I test it to find out how much calcite it contains. A high content of calcite in the river means that caves may be forming upstream.

can cause broken bones or other injuries that can leave a person unable to get out of a cave without help. There's also the risk of being trapped when rocks fall or when a sudden rainstorm causes a cave to flood. Because I'm small physically, I can squeeze through spaces most other people can't. I have put my small size to good use as a member of the "Tiny Team"—a group of volunteers specially trained to rescue fellow cavers stuck in very tight places. I have taken part in several underground rescue operations. For me, it's like taking care of family. The caving community is tight; we look after our own. If someone's hurt, you want to be there for them. And you know they will be there for you.

Another advantage of being able to wiggle into narrow crawlways is that I get to investigate a lot of new stuff. My husband, Brent, and I and some other caving friends have adopted several TAG caves as special projects. We probe for new passages, called leads, and survey and map what we find. Mapping a cave helps us establish how a cave system was born and how it ties into the land around it. One of our goals is to figure out the hydrological, or water, connection between all the caves on Fox Mountain in Dade County, Georgia. To do this we use dye tracing, a technique that would be particularly useful when Hazel and I explored the underwater caves of Mexico's Yucatán Peninsula with the IMAX theatre film crew.

Caving not only fulfills my need to explore, it lets me push the limits to see what I can accomplish physically. Squeezing through tight spaces like this, for example, is a fun challenge. If my head fits, so will the rest of me.

Caving Underwater

The limestone caves Nancy and I encountered when we traveled to Mexico's Yucatán Peninsula were different from anything either of us had ever experienced. They are much more hazardous to explore. That's because most of the caves in the Yucatán are flooded by underground streams. There's only one way to investigate the underwater chambers, and that's to put on scuba gear and dive.

Ever since I became a caver I have wanted to explore underwater caves, even though I know that cave diving is considered to be one of the world's most dangerous sports. The caver in me wants to see

Known as cenotes (say-NO-tayz), water-filled sinkholes (above) supplied the ancient Maya people with water for their cities. To divers today, they serve as the doorway to incredible underwater caves (left).

where the water-filled passages lead. The scientist in me is lured by their research potential. In some of the Yucatán caves, there is a mysterious zone where fresh water from underground rivers meets—but does not mix with—salt water from the sea. It's called the halocline. Because the halocline is a boundary between two extremes, it seemed likely to me that it would support microorganisms that don't exist anywhere else. The thought of finding the halocline was exciting. I couldn't wait to get started.

Before I could begin the search, I had to devote myself to learning how to cave dive. Most cave diving accidents are caused by inexperience. If you're not properly trained, your first cave dive could well be your last. The sport is especially dangerous in the area where we were filming. There are no air pockets in these caves. They are completely submerged, so you can't just pop up to the surface if something goes wrong, the way you can in open-water diving. Usually the only way out is back through the entrance of the cave. If you kick up the silt on the floor of the cave, it can cloud the water and make it impossible to see anything—including the way out. You can't tell up from down, so it's easy to become disoriented and confused in an underwater cave.

I already had some scuba experience, so I jumped at the chance to learn cave diving. MacGillivray Freeman Films arranged for Dan Lins, one of the world's most experienced cave diving instructors, to teach me the special techniques and safety procedures I needed to master before I could collect samples from the halocline. After many training dives, I was prepared to tackle the underwater caves we would explore for the movie.

The Yucatán Peninsula is mostly composed of limestone karst covered with a layer of lush jungle foliage. Scattered throughout are hundreds of water-filled sinkholes called cenotes. Some cenotes are as large as lakes, and many are very deep. Cenotes are created when underground rivers weaken the overlying limestone and cause it to collapse, creating holes. These holes become filled with

Reeling out a dive line, I swim through Jaguar Cave in our first attempt to find a halocline. Our time in the cave was limited. We had to head for the exit when one-third of the air in our tanks was gone to ensure we'd have enough air if problems arose on the way out.

To the ancient Maya people, the cenotes were sacred gateways used by spirits of the dead to enter the underworld.

water as the underground streams flow through the karst on their way to the sea. The winding, horizontal channels formed by the streams connect to form a vast underwater cave system. To the ancient Maya people, the cenotes were sacred gateways used by spirits of the dead to enter the underworld. Today, cave divers respect them as the doorways to some of the world's most spectacular caves.

Our Mexican guides, Ruben and Jorge, led us through the jungle to a cenote known as Jaguar Cave, where we hoped to find an uncontaminated halocline. Nancy and I decided to use a scientific method known as dye tracing to see where the cave connected with the ocean. This would give us an idea of where to find the halocline. We poured an environmentally safe, nonstaining dye solution made of a chemical called fluorescein into the water at the entrance

Stripped-down trucks called Buddymobiles (above) hauled us through the jungle to the cenotes. As we headed across a cenote (right) and down to the cave entrance, we used motorized scooters to save energy and time.

of the cave. Then we headed to a lagoon downstream to the spot where we suspected the cave met the sea. I dove underwater to retrieve the charcoal packet I had placed there earlier. When Nancy examined it with a black light, she detected the fluorescent dye. Success! The cave connected with the sea right where we suspected it would.

I checked out Jaguar Cave for myself the next day. Jorge and Joel Tower, an experienced cave diver, accompanied me, as did the MFF film crew. Once all the cameras, lights, air tanks, and other equipment vital to filmmaking and diving were in place, we did a final safety check then dove into the waters of the cave.

We swam through a passage that opened into a room with stunning formations, including stalactites and stalagmites. These speleothems, which could only have formed above water, are

Like many full-time cave dwellers, this fish lacks eyes. But when you live in total darkness, who needs eyes?

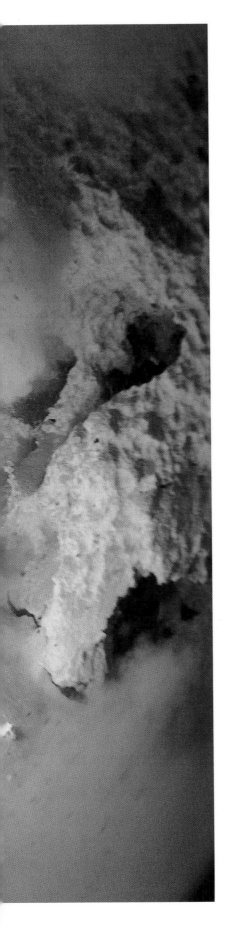

evidence that the underwater caves of the Yucatán were once dry. When the last ice age ended some 15,000 years ago, melting glaciers caused the sea level to rise and flood the caves.

As we made our way farther into the cave, the passages narrowed. Our movement stirred up silt that blinded my view. This made me very nervous because silt can take hours, even days, to settle. Thanks to my training, I knew where to find the dive line—the nylon string we attached to the entrance of the cave and reeled out as we swam. The dive line will lead you out of a cave if your light fails or if you become confused—or blinded by silt. The cave became too small for us to continue our search for the halocline. Although the fluorescein dye had made it through, we could not. It was time to turn around.

We were back to square one. Fortunately, we had heard about another cenote that was supposed to be enormous. We thought we might find a halocline there because the cenote was part of a chain that headed toward the sea. No one knew exactly where the cenote was, so Nancy took to the air to find it. Flying over the jungle in a small airplane, she spotted the cenote and used a global positioning system (GPS) to determine its latitude and longitude.

When stirred-up silt in Jaguar Cave (left) blinded our view, we used the dive line to find our way out. Since we did not find a halocline there, we decided to try another cenote, which Nancy helped locate (above).

Back at camp, she plotted the coordinates on a map, which we used to guide us through the jungle. The cenote was so huge that Jorge named it El Jefe. That's Spanish for "the boss." Supposedly it linked to a cenote downstream called Lost Worlds.

To save energy and time, we used motorized scooters to explore the cave below El Jefe. We didn't find a halocline in it, but the cave did connect with Lost Worlds cenote, so we surfaced there. Nancy and Ruben were waiting for us with fresh air tanks on a small island in the cenote. Nancy was concerned that I was pushing myself too hard. She and I both had friends who had lost their lives cave diving. I assured her that I was just fine.

Joel glides around fragile formations, as we hunt for the halocline in El Jefe cenote. Like many cave divers, he wears his air tanks mounted on either side of his body, not on his back like traditional open-sea divers do. This allows him to squeeze through narrow passages.

Success! We finally find the halocline. I collect a sample so that we can share our discovery with Nancy and the others.

The scooters, however, were running out of juice. From this point on we'd have to swim. After strapping on the fresh air tanks, we plunged back into Lost Worlds and followed the current downstream into a tunnel.

Shining my flashlight to light the way, I noticed that the water ahead was shimmering. We had finally found the halocline. It was beautiful! The top layer of fresh water was sky blue; the bottom layer of seawater was deep turquoise blue. The silvery halocline glistened between the two layers. I swam right into it and collected a sample in a tube. Maybe the creatures in the halocline would help

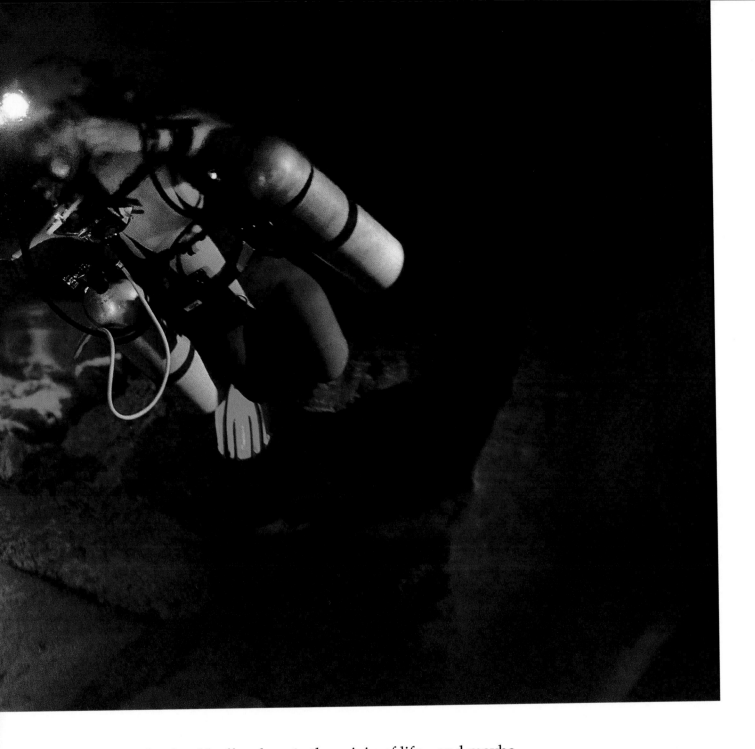

save lives, maybe they'd offer clues to the origin of life—and maybe they'd lead nowhere. All I knew was that I was thrilled to have found a place where we would be able to collect microorganisms to study. Soon I would be returning to my lab in Colorado, where my co-workers would be as excited as I was about my find. I look forward to the time when we will have samples to study to see what secrets the halocline "bugs" might contain.

As we prepared to leave the Yucatán, Nancy and I reflected on all we had seen and learned during our adventures. We realized more than ever the need to preserve all of Earth's underground realms.

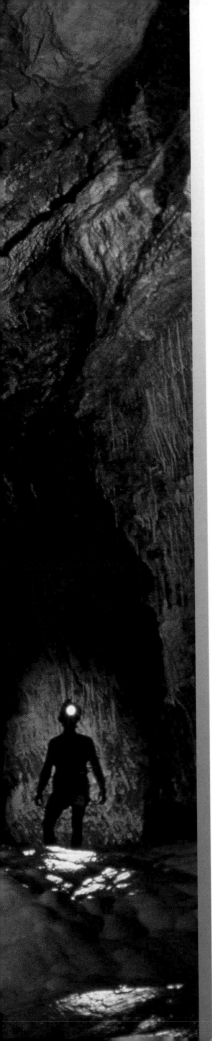

Caring for Caves

The love we share for Earth's caves makes us passionate about protecting them. The underground world is a unique scientific resource and a place of incredible beauty. It is also a very fragile environment that can be easily damaged. Caves are a nonrenewable natural resource. Unlike a forest that can be replanted with trees, caves can never be replaced once they have been harmed.

Caves face two main threats. The first is pollution. Polluted water from farms or industries can seep underground into caves, carrying chemicals that can stop the growth of formations and kill the various life-forms that live there. Many cave creatures, including some kinds of cave shrimp and salamanders, are already on the verge of extinction. Another form of pollution comes from people dumping trash—everything from household garbage to old refrigerators and dead animals—in sinkholes and at cave entrances. This not only dirties the caves but also can contaminate drinking water that comes from underground streams.

Hidden River Cave, which lies beneath the town of Horse Cave, Kentucky, is an example of a cave that was almost destroyed by pollution. The underground river flowing through the cave supplied the town's drinking water until the 1940s, when it became too polluted to drink. For the next 45 years, Hidden River Cave was basically used as a sewer. Luckily, there's a happy ending to this story. In 1989 a new sewage treatment plant was built to keep contaminated waters out of the cave. Then cave conservationists began cleaning up the cave, removing all the trash that had been dumped in it. Their efforts were so successful that today Hidden River Cave is open to the public for tours.

New Mexico's Lechuguilla Cave contains many unusual formations, such as these 50-foot-tall calcite columns. To protect the cave from outside contamination, only authorized cavers are allowed to enter it.

Take nothing but pictures, kill nothing but time, leave nothing but footprints.

Gypsum "beards" (below) and calcite "cave pearls" (right) are among the delicate decorations in Lechuguilla Cave.

Human visitors are the second major threat to caves. A careless caver can destroy in an instant what took hundreds of thousands of years to form. Careful cavers keep these guidelines in mind:

- Behave as a guest in a cave. Respect its creatures by not disturbing them, and respect its formations by not touching them.

- Don't take anything from a cave as a souvenir. This includes fossils and bones as well as formations.

- Don't leave anything in a cave that you took in with you.

- Follow the motto of the National Speleological Society: "Take nothing but pictures, kill nothing but time, leave nothing but footprints."

Caves hold many marvelous mysteries. If we can preserve caves from harm, then future generations of cavers can help solve these mysteries. Perhaps you will be the caver who discovers an amazing new cave system, or the researcher who finds a unique cave "bug" that holds the key to curing a deadly disease. As long as there are caves, the possibilities are endless.

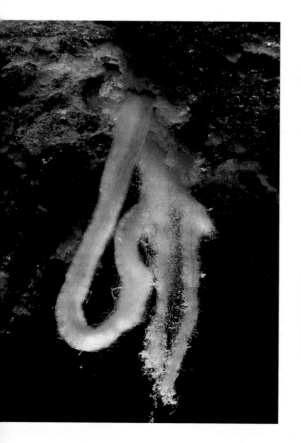

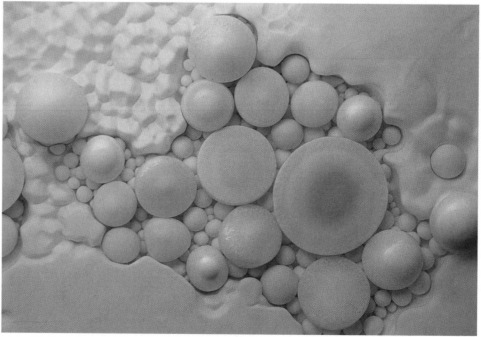

Whether nestled high above the Grand Canyon (right) or hidden beneath the surface, all caves are priceless treasures that deserve respect and protection.

Glossary

Bacteria
a kind of microscopic, single-celled organism

Cave
a naturally formed hole underground that is usually connected to the surface and big enough for a person to enter. Caves are sometimes called caverns.

Cenote
a deep hole in limestone with water at the bottom that is found in Mexico's Yucatán region

Column
a cave formation, or speleothem, that forms when a stalactite and a stalagmite join

Crevasse
a deep, wedge-shaped opening in a glacier

DNA
a long molecule that stores genetic information. The initials stand for deoxyribonucleic acid.

Echolocation
a system by which an animal, such as a bat, determines the position of an object by sending out sound waves that bounce back when they hit the object

Geology
the scientific study of the physical history of Earth, including its formation, makeup, and the forces that change it

Glacier
a huge mass of ice that moves slowly over land

Ice age
any long period of time when glaciers cover large parts of Earth's land

Karst
a region underlain by limestone that is honeycombed with sinkholes, underground streams, and caves

Limestone
a kind of rock that is formed over time mainly from layers of tiny sea animals and plants. Most of the world's caves form in limestone.

Microbiology
the scientific study of microscopic organisms

Microorganism
an organism so small it cannot be seen without a microscope. Bacteria are microorganisms.

Organism
any living thing, including plants, animals, and bacteria

Sinkhole
a circular depression in the ground that forms where limestone collapses; sometimes the entrance to a cave

Speleology
the scientific study of caves

Speleothem
a rock formation created by deposits left by mineral-rich water dripping or seeping into a cave

Spelunker
a person who likes to explore caves

Stalactite
a speleothem that hangs down from a cave ceiling

Stalagmite
a speleothem that builds up from a cave floor

Tyrolean traverse
a method of crossing a crevasse or canyon using a tight, horizontally positioned rope

Resources

If you want to see if caving is for you, the best place to start is with a show cave—a cave that is operated by guides and open to tourists. To learn if there are any show caves near you, write the National Caves Association, 4138 Dark Hollow Road, McMinnville, Tennessee 37110, or check out their Web site at www.cavern.com.

If you want to try caving for real someday, your best bet is to contact the National Speleological Society (NSS), 2813 Cave Avenue, Huntsville, Alabama 35810-4431. Or, you can go to its Web site at www.caves.org. The NSS can direct you to an organized caving club, called a grotto, near you. A grotto can help you find someone to teach you how to cave safely. Some grottos may even have special caving trips that are open to families.

Warning!
Are you ready to grab a flashlight and head underground? Stop right where you are! Although caving can be an amazing adventure, it can also be dangerous, even deadly, especially for inexperienced cavers. That's why you should NEVER enter a cave unless you are with an experienced adult caver.

This map shows the maze of karst areas underlying North America. Sites where Hazel and Nancy had their caving adventures are indicated by red diamonds.

Index

Illustrations are indicated in **boldface.** If illustrations are included within a page span the entire span is in **boldface.**

For Nancy and me it is always exciting to find a new cave to explore. Here I work my way down to one in the Grand Canyon.

Dedications

For Mom and Dad, who gave me their passion for caves and caving, for my brothers, Oliver and Chris, who taught me how to be tough and never called me a sissy, and for my very own Cave Man, Brent, with love to infinity plus one —NHA

To my mentors Dan Lins, Jim Moon, Norman Pace, and Michael Vasil, and to my grandfather, Michael Morris, who never let me believe anything was beyond my grasp—HAB

For Allie and David—MFD

Published by the National Geographic Society

John M. Fahey, Jr., *President and Chief Executive Officer*
Gilbert M. Grosvenor, *Chairman of the Board*
Nina D. Hoffman, *Senior Vice President*
William R. Gray, *Vice President and Director, Book Division*

Staff for this book

Nancy Laties Feresten
Publishing Director,
Children's Books

Suzanne Patrick Fonda
Project Editor

Lori Rick
Project Manager
MacGillivray Freeman Films

Melissa G. Ryan
Illustrations Editor

Marianne Koszorus
Design Director

Dorrit Green
Designer

Art Palmer
Professor of Hydrology
State University of New York
Science Consultant

Carl Mehler
Director of Maps

Meredith C. Wilcox
Illustrations Assistant

Ann K. McCain
Indexer

Lewis R. Bassford
Production Manager

R. Gary Colbert
Production Director

Vincent P. Ryan
Manufacturing Manager

Illustration Credits

All photographs in this book are from MacGillivray Freeman Films unless otherwise noted:

2–3, 6, 7, Bill Hatcher; 13, 18–19, Chris Blum; 20–21, 21, John Burcham; 22 (upper), Dr. Charles Elzinga, Michigan State University; 24, Chris Blum; 26–27, Harris Photographic; 28, Courtesy Hazel Barton; 29, Harris Photographic; 32–33, Alan Cressler; 34, Courtesy Cato & Susan Holler; 34–35, 36, 37, Alan Cressler; 38–39, 40, 41, John Burcham; 42–43, Alan Cressler; 45, 48, 48–49, 51, Bill Hatcher; 56–57, Michael Nichols/NGS Image Collection; 58 (both), Michael Nichols, National Geographic Photographer; 59, 62, John Burcham; back cover, Bill Hatcher

Published by the National Geographic Society
1145 17th Street, N.W.
Washington, D.C. 20036-4688

Text is set in Palatino, photo legends in Clair, and chapter headings in Allise.

Library of Congress
Cataloging-in-Publication Data

Aulenbach, Nancy Holler.
  Exploring caves : journeys into the earth / by Nancy Holler Aulenbach and Hazel A. Barton, with Marfé Ferguson Delano.
      p. cm.
      ISBN 0-7922-7721-X (hc.)
      1. Caving–Juvenile literature. 2. Spelunkers–Biography–Juvenile literature. [1. Caving. 2. Caves.] I. Barton, Hazel A. II. Delano, Marfé Ferguson.
      GV200.62 .A82 2001
      796.52'5–dc21   00-055410

Printed in the U.S.A.

The world's largest nonprofit scientific and educational organization, the National Geographic Society was founded in 1888 "for the increase and diffusion of geographic knowledge." Fulfilling this mission, the Society educates and inspires millions every day through magazines, books, television programs, videos, maps and atlases, research grants, the National Geographic Bee, teacher workshops, and innovative classroom materials. The Society is supported through membership dues and income from the sale of its educational products.

Call 1-800-NGS-LINE (647-5463) for more information.

Visit our Web site:
www.nationalgeographic.com